PICTURESQUE
DORSET
A PHOTOGRAPHIC SOUVENIR IN BEAUTIFUL COLOUR

SALMON

Situated in a peaceful valley enclosed by wooded slopes, Milton Abbas is a neatly planned 18th century estate village. To protect his privacy at nearby Milton Abbey, the Earl of Dorchester demolished the old houses and had the village rebuilt on its present site.

This pretty thatched cottage was the birthplace in 1840 of Thomas Hardy and here he wrote some of his best-known novels. Tucked away in the hamlet of Higher Bockhampton, it lies on the edge of the wild and primitive moorland which features in his books as Egdon Heath.

At the southern end of Studland Bay is the spit of land called The Foreland, off which stand the isolated chalk stacks known as Old Harry Rocks. Prominent landmarks, Old Harry and Old Harry's Wife have been eroded from the cliffs by the action of the wind and waves.

The popular resort of Swanage lies at the southern end of a semicircular sandy bay which saw a famous victory by King Alfred over a Danish fleet in 877 AD. Today it offers a safe bathing beach and good anchorage for yachts including the occasional visiting tall ship.

Facing the great sweep of Lyme Bay, West Bay is a popular little resort with a harbour built in 1740 to serve inland Bridport. Here the impressive cliffs are worn into a series of ledges by the effect of erosion on the alternating bands of hard and soft rock.

Easily reached by a pleasant coast walk from Bridport or West Bay is Burton Bradstock, a delightfully unspoiled example of a rural Dorset village.
Its narrow, twisting lanes are lined with picturesque thatched cottages which make the village an immense attraction for artists and visitors.

The ancient town of Sherborne has many notable buildings including the splendid Abbey Church. The present structure, dating mainly from the 15th century, replaced an earlier one and retains a fine Saxon doorway as well as a tenor bell given to the abbey by Cardinal Wolsey.

One of the most famous and picturesque landmarks in the ancient market town of Shaftesbury is Gold Hill. This ancient cobbled street, lined with pretty tiled and thatched cottages, leads steeply down from the present day High Street affording splendid views over Blackmoor Vale.

In times gone by Weymouth was a major port, and the harbour, a target for considerable bombing during the Second World War, has always been a lively centre of activity. Today fishing boats and pleasure craft still mingle with commercial vessels, and a regular ferry service operates to the Channel Islands.

Weymouth is one of the principal resorts on the south coast, boasting a long sweeping sandy beach, a fine promenade and a busy harbour. Seen here in Weymouth harbour, the *Queen Galadriel*, a magnificent two-masted sailing ship, was built in 1937 and originally worked as a Baltic trader.

Dominated by the majestic ruins of its castle, strategically sited in a gap in the Purbeck Hills, the ancient village of Corfe Castle is built of local grey Purbeck stone. The present castle dates from the 15th century and has been in ruins since it was blown up during the Civil War.

The ancient market town of Wareham has been important since Saxon times owing to its situation at the head of the River Frome which runs into Poole harbour. A popular centre for fishermen and small-boat enthusiasts, the quay always presents a scene of bustling activity.

Set below steep hills, the narrow streets of elegant Lyme Regis look out across a wide sweeping bay. No longer a commercial port, the attractive harbour, protected by the 14th century stone breakwater known as The Cobb, is still used by fishing boats and private craft.

Seen here from Golden Cap, which at 626 feet is the highest point on England's southern coast, the village of Seatown has a beach of golden sand and shingle. It is backed by high sandstone cliffs which are subject to constant erosion by the wind and waves.

Connected to the mainland by a narrow neck of land, the peninsula of Portland culminates at Portland Bill. Here the 136 feet high lighthouse, built in the early years of the 20th century to replace previous structures, warns shipping from dangerous channels and tidal currents.

Dorset's chalk downs meet the sea at Lulworth in an impressive stretch of coastline where the high white cliffs are indented with sandy coves. Lulworth Cove, one of England's most photographed spots, is nearly circular in shape with a narrow, well-protected entrance.

Situated on the open, sandy expanse of Wareham Heath, the Blue Pool has been declared a Site of Special Scientific Interest because of its varied animal and plant life. The pool, surrounded by pine trees, occupies the site of an old clay pit which gives the water its intense colour.

West of famous Lulworth Cove is the spectacular natural arch of rock known as Durdle Door. Standing 40 feet high, it was created over a period of time by the action of the sea which wears away the soft rock to leave an arch of harder Portland stone.

The attractive village of Wool stands on the River Frome, surrounded by water-meadows and heathland. It has a fine 17th century bridge, and Elizabethan Woolbridge Manor was used by Thomas Hardy in *Tess of the D'Urbervilles* as the setting for her wedding night.

Dorchester is still a bustling market town today as it was when it featured as Casterbridge in Thomas Hardy's novels. A number of interesting old buildings can be seen in High West Street, including the The Old Crown Court where the trial of the Tolpuddle Martyrs took place in 1834.

Seen here from the 19th century folly known as Clavell's Tower, Kimmeridge Bay is a lonely cove which was once associated with smugglers. Below the dark cliffs is a shingle beach broken by rocky ledges which provide a rich habitat for marine life.

The promontory of Worbarrow Tout projects into the sea at the eastern edge of Worbarrow Bay, providing superb views of Dorset's dramatic coastal scenery. The cliffs, consisting of contrasting bands of the different Purbeck strata, are of great interest to geologists.

Famous for its six-arched medieval bridge across the River Stour, Sturminster Newton is an outstandingly attractive village situated on the southern edge of Blackmoor Vale. The Old Mill, one of two mills in the village, stands in a beautiful setting on the banks of the river.

Evershot is one of a number of delightful little villages which nestle among wooded hills south of Yeovil. In Hardy's novel *Tess of the D'Urbervilles*, the heroine breakfasted at this thatched cottage, now known as Tess Cottage, on her way to Emminster.

Best known for its white hillside figure of the Cerne Giant, the village of Cerne Abbas is itself exceptionally beautiful. Among its many interesting old buildings is the gatehouse of the 10th century abbey, at one time one of the most important in the south of England.

There are many theories about the origin of the massive chalk figure known as the Cerne Giant. Measuring 180 feet from head to toe, it is thought by some to be an ancient fertility symbol, but recent research suggests that it may have been created in the 17th century to satirize Oliver Cromwell.

Situated on a magnificent bay, Bournemouth is one of the country's leading resorts, well known for its spacious parks, gardens and open spaces. Along with the Lower and Upper Gardens, the attractive Central Gardens extend along the little Bourne valley to the seafront.

Among Bournemouth's many attractions are its sands, cliffs and wooded chines cut into the cliffs which provide shady paths down to the beach. With its fine Victorian pier and International Centre, the resort is popular for conferences as well as with holiday-makers.

Christchurch is a tranquil town which takes its name from its 11th century priory church which stands behind the quay. Situated between the estuaries of the Rivers Avon and Stour, the sheltered harbour offers safe moorings for yachts and other small boats.

Situated just east of Bournemouth, the little resort of Southbourne has a sand and shingle beach sheltered by steep cliffs. The promontory of Hengistbury Head, a popular observation point for bird migrations, can be seen to the east, curving around Christchurch harbour.

Originally founded as a nunnery in 713, beautiful Wimborne Minster dominates the peaceful market town of Wimborne. The building embraces many architectural styles and among its items of historical interest include an astronomical clock believed to date from 1325.

Situated on one of the largest shallow-water anchorages in Britain, Poole has always been an important port and it is now also a popular resort.
The heart of the town centres around the harbour where there are numerous buildings of historic interest, including the splendid Custom House.

An important market town from early times, Blandford Forum was largely destroyed by fire in 1731 and the rebuilt town is an outstanding example of Georgian architecture. The imposing buildings around the market place were the work of two brothers who were local builders.

The beautiful gardens at Compton Acres, overlooking Poole harbour, are reputed to be some of the finest in Europe. Containing many rare plants and some splendid statuary, this charming Italian garden is one of seven areas created in English and foreign styles.

Eastwards from Bournemouth overlooking the wide sweep of Poole Bay, Boscombe is joined to its busy neighbour by a promenade and cliff drive. A popular resort in its own right, Boscombe has fine sands, splendid gardens and a 750 feet long pier which first opened in 1889.